Discover India
State by State

OFF TO MEGHALAYA

SONIA MEHTA

PUFFIN BOOKS
An imprint of Penguin Random House

PUFFIN BOOKS

USA | Canada | UK | Ireland | Australia | New Zealand | India | South Africa | China | Singapore

Puffin Books is part of the Penguin Random House group of companies whose addresses can be found at global.penguinrandomhouse.com

Published by Penguin Random House India Pvt. Ltd
4th Floor, Capital Tower 1, MG Road,
Gurugram 122 002, Haryana, India

First published in Puffin Books by Penguin Random House India 2018

Picture Credits

P 8: Clouded leopard (© Ltshears [CC BY-SA 3.0 (https://creativecommons.org/licenses/by-sa/3.0)], from Wikimedia Commons); p 9: Gamhar (© LRBurdak [GFDL (http://www.gnu.org/copyleft/fdl.html) or CC-BY-SA-3.0 (http://creativecommons.org/licenses/by-sa/3.0/)], from Wikimedia Commons); P 10: Cherrapunji (© RMehra [GFDL (http://www.gnu.org/copyleft/fdl.html) or CC-BY-SA-3.0 (http://creativecommons.org/licenses/by-sa/3.0/)], via Wikimedia Commons), Tura Peak (© Tejan A Momin), P 11: Nongstoin (© Joist John L Nonglait [CC BY-SA 4.0 (https://creativecommons.org/licenses/by-sa/4.0)], from Wikimedia Commons), Nongpoh (©http://ribhoi.gov.in/photos/marngar.jpg), Jowai (© Arindam Das [CC BY-SA 4.0 (https://creativecommons.org/licenses/by-sa/4.0)], from Wikimedia Commons); P 13: Nature made Shiv ling in Mawjymbuin Cave (© Sharada Prasad CS (Flickr: CSP_4312.JPG) [CC BY 2.0 (https://creativecommons.org/licenses/by/2.0)], via Wikimedia Commons); P 24: A band in Shillong (© Vikas gupta70 [GFDL (http://www.gnu.org/copyleft/fdl.html) or CC-BY-SA-3.0 (http://creativecommons.org/licenses/by-sa/3.0/)], via Wikimedia Commons); P 30: Wangala dance of Garo community (David Talukdar/Shutterstock.com); P 38: Christ the Redeemer, Brazil (Mark Schwettmann/Shutterstock.com); P 39: The Little Mermaid, Copenhagen (Pocholo Calapre/Shutterstock.com); P 40: Umngot river (© Vikramjit Kakati [CC BY-SA 4.0 (https://creativecommons.org/licenses/by-sa/4.0)], from Wikimedia Common)

The views and opinions expressed in this book are the author's own and the facts are as reported by her, which have been verified to the extent possible, and the publishers are not in any way liable for the same.

The information in this book is based on research from bona fide sites and published books and is true to the best of the author's knowledge at the time of going to print. The author is not responsible for any further changes or developments occurring post the publication of this book. This series is not a comprehensive representation of the states of India but is intended to give children a flavour of the lifestyles and cultures of different states. All illustrations are artistic representations only.

ISBN 9780143440932

Design and layout by Quadrum Solutions Pvt. Ltd
Printed at Repro India Limited

www.penguin.co.in

This is a legitimate digitally printed version of the book and therefore might not have certain extra finishing on the cover.

Hello Kids!

I'm so happy you are reading this book. India is an incredible country and there are lots of things about it that we never get to hear about.

I discovered India because my father was in the Indian army. He was posted to many places all over India—and we dutifully followed him. Can you imagine that by the time I was in the tenth standard, I had changed nine schools? Of course it was hard making new friends almost every year, but the good part was that I got to live in so many places. Right from Kerala, where I was born, to Kashmir, Jhansi, Shillong, Chandigarh, Goa . . . the list is long.

Every time I go to a new place, I feel amazed at how different each state is from the other—and yet, how similar. Did you know that we can see monuments from the Stone Age right here in India? Or that we have more than twenty official languages, and most Indians know three or four on an average? Or even that some of the world's most amazing scientific marvels were invented in India?

Oh, there are many, many, many fun and fantastic things about the states of India, which we simply must get to know.

So get your backpack ready, get set to meet some new friends and join me on a fun trip as we DISCOVER INDIA, STATE BY STATE.

I hope you enjoy reading this book as much as I have enjoyed writing it. I would love to hear from you. So do write to me at sonia.mehta@quadrumltd.com.

Lots of love,
Sonia Aunty

Mishki and Pushka have come to visit Earth from their home planet, Zoomba. They have never seen such an amazing place. Zoomba doesn't have trees and mountains and rivers like Earth does. But the people look exactly the same. When they come to Earth, they meet a sweet old man whom they call Daadu Dolma. Daadu Dolma shows them all the wonderful places in India and tells Mishki and Pushka all about them.

Mishki and Pushka can't believe what they see. They have seen a lot of Earth, but they have never, ever seen a place like India.

They are off to explore India state by state :)

Mishki

Mishki is a curious little girl. She is always asking loads of questions. On her home planet, she is always getting into trouble for poking her nose into things that are not her business.

Pushka

Pushka is Mishki's brother. He loves adventure. He is always ready to try a new challenge. Whether it's climbing a mountain, or diving into a cold, cold sea, he is up for it.

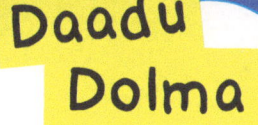

Daadu Dolma

Daadu Dolma is a wise old man who has lived on Earth longer than the mountains and seas. No one knows quite how old he is, but he certainly has been around. He knows everything about everything.

Pushka is packing his bag. He wants to know what he must carry with him on this trip to the state of Meghalaya.

'Pushka,' says Daadu, 'the one thing you must remember to carry to Meghalaya is your umbrella. And if you have them, carry a raincoat and gumboots as well.'

'But why, Daadu?' Mishki asks curiously. 'Does it rain so much there?'

Yes,' replies Daadu. 'Meghalaya is one of the wettest regions in the whole world. So we'd better be prepared.'

'What else will we get to see?' Mishki is demands.

'Mountains, hills, rivers, forests and lovely wildlife,' replies Daadu.

Mishki and Pushka rush to get ready. They can't wait. They are

OFF TO MEGHALAYA!!!

A SNEAK PEEK

LAND AHOY!
About the land, water, rivers, mountains and seas.
page 6

LONG, LONG AGO
The story of the state.
page 14

TALK TIME
What language do the people speak?
page 20

A PEEP INTO THEIR LIFE
The music, dance and lifestyle of the people.
page 22

BRICKS AND STONES
Of houses, buildings and bridges.
page 32

STANDING STRONG
Famous monuments in Meghalaya.
page 34

WORKING HARD
What work do people do?
page 40

YUM YUM YUM
Food, food, food. What's the yummy food of Meghalaya?
page 44

WHAT TO WEAR?
The clothes they wear.
page 48

AUTOGRAPH, PLEASE?
Famous people—past and present.
page 50

ONCE UPON A TIME . . .
Stories from the state.
page 52

Land ahoy!

Where exactly is Meghalaya, Daadu?

Meghalaya is in the north-eastern part of India. It once used to be a part of the state of Assam.

ONE OF THE SEVEN SISTERS

Meghalaya is a tiny state that is one of the seven states in the north-east of India called the Seven Sisters. Its other sisters are Assam, Tripura, Nagaland, Manipur, Mizoram and Sikkim. But all these are not its neighbours. It has only two close neighbours— Assam and Bangladesh.

Assam

Meghalaya

Bangladesh

ON THE MAP

To see exactly where MEGHALAYA is on the map of India, go to http://www.mapsofindia.com/maps/india/india-political-map.htm

THE HILLS ARE ALIVE

Meghalaya is basically a mountain-like plateau with stunning scenery. It is part of the Deccan Plateau—the bit that became detached from the main plateau. There are three main hills in this area—the Garo Hills, the Khasi Hills and the Jaintia Hills. They form a massive tableland with lots of ridges and valleys in between.

Meghalaya means 'where the clouds live'. A perfect name, because it is often cloudy in Meghalaya with lots and lots of rain.

Khasi Hills

Garo Hills

Jaintia Hills

WATER WATER

The large plateau goes suddenly down a steep slope, right down to the lowlands of Bangladesh. There are many streams and rivers that flow out of the plateau and find their way down the slopes. The Umiam Badapani Lake is an important one. It not only irrigates farms, but also provides hydroelectric power to Meghalaya and Assam.

RHYME TIME

Meghalaya, as we've seen, is a land of clouds. Mishki is writing a poem about clouds. Help her out by finding six words rhyming with cloud in the word grid.

G	P	R	O	U	D	F	D	S	A
V	O	W	E	D	C	X	C	V	B
C	C	O	W	E	D	W	X	F	Q
V	V	C	R	O	W	D	D	E	S
Z	X	V	B	A	L	O	U	D	A
L	O	U	D	N	M	Z	A	S	D
A	C	B	O	W	E	D	Z	X	C
P	L	O	U	G	H	E	D	Q	S

Pine Forest

FOREST FANTASY

This cold and wet weather is fantastic for many kinds of trees. There is a big blanket of forests covering most of Meghalaya. There are lush forests that have trees like pine, sal and bamboo. There are also other types of trees like oak, birch, beech and magnolia trees.

WET WET WET

The climate in Meghalaya is quite cool all through the year. But . . . watch out for that cloudburst! Parts of Meghalaya are very wet indeed. Cherrapunji in Meghalaya is said to be among the world's wettest areas. In fact, it's only during winter, from December to February, that one can hope for some dry days. So a visit to Cherrapunji means carrying along plenty of rainwear.

Clouded Leopard

WILD WONDER

Think of deep forests and you think of wild animals roaming in them. And sure enough, there is plenty of wildlife in Meghalaya. Tigers, clouded leopards, wild boars, deer, wild bison, snakes, squirrels and many more animals roam these forests. There are plenty of birds too. Peacocks, parrots, hornbills, partridges, jungle fowls and mynas are just a few.

FUN FACTS

State animal
Clouded Leopard

State bird
Hill Myna

State flower
Lady Slipper Orchid

State tree
Gamhar

FOREST SAFARI

Mishki loves peacocks. Pushka wants to meet a tiger. And Daadu Dolma wants to spot a leopard. Can you help each of them get to their animal of choice?

Hornbill

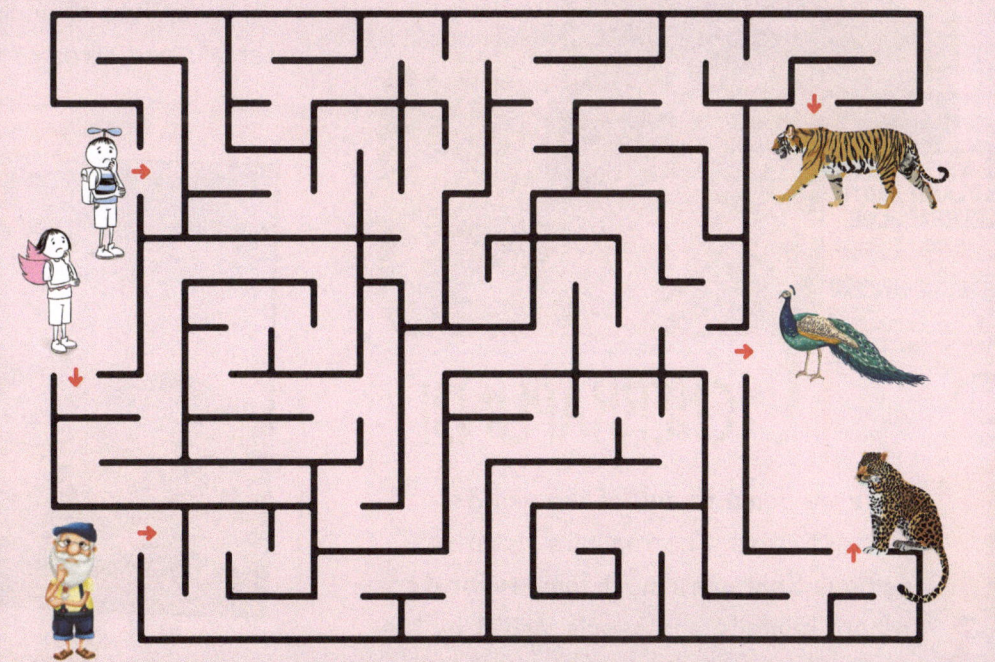

CITY CITY BANG BANG

SHILLONG

When the British ruled India, they fell in love with Shillong's rolling hills. They called it the 'Scotland of the East'. Today, it is the capital of Meghalaya and is a busy, bustling city. Shillong is also known as the rock capital of India—that's how popular rock music is there.

Scotland of the east

TURA

This hilly town is one of Meghalaya's larger towns. Sitting prettily in the Tura valley with the Tura peak smiling down on it, it has lots of undiscovered trails, waterfalls and streams to be explored.

CHERRAPUNJI

Here we come to one of the world's wettest cities. Cherrapunji's historical name is Sohra. It's most famous for its record rainfalls, and people visit it by the hundreds to experience its natural beauty.

Tura peak

NONGSTOIN

This tiny town is the headquarters of the western part of the Khasi Hills. It's at quite a height. The famous Longshiang Falls are close by and a major tourist attraction.

Longshiang Falls

NONGPOH

This town is at the centre of a district called Ri-Bhoi. Unlike the rest of this state, Nongpoh can sometimes get warm and sticky, because it is rather close to the massive Brahmaputra plain. The Ri-Bhoi area is full of orchards growing pineapples, bananas, papayas and litchis.

JOWAI

This beautiful town is a busy student town with lots of colleges and universities. Students from all over Meghalaya as well as some neighbouring states come here for their education.

WONDERS OF NATURE

There are many natural (and some man-made) wonders that people come from far and wide to enjoy in Meghalaya. Not surprising considering the location with its mountains, valleys, slopes, streams, rivers and lakes.

TEE TIME

Shillong has a natural golf course that is Meghalaya's pride. It is one of Asia's largest golf courses and is known as the 'Gleneagle of the East'. It's spread across a valley that is full of pine and rhododendron trees. People come to play golf here from all over the world.

FALL FOR THE WATERFALLS

There are some stunning waterfalls in Meghalaya, with lovely names, that can leave you awestruck. The Elephant Falls, the Bishop and Beadon Falls, the Spread Eagle Falls and the Sweet Falls are just some of Meghalaya's waterfalls that come crashing down the mountainsides. Located near Shillong, these falls draw thousands of visitors every year.

Elephant Falls

CAVING IN

Meghalaya has many mysterious caves too. People go exploring these caves, in a sport called caving. To enter the Krem Mawkhyrdop caves, you have to wade through a river that suddenly dips into a dark and mysterious cave. The Krem Dam cave on the other hand has a wide open entrance where a mountainside must have collapsed at some point. The Krem Mawjymbuin cave has a large stalactite-and-stalagmite structure that reminds people of a *Shiv ling*. Oh, going caving in Meghalaya can be exciting all right!

Stalagmite structure of a Shiv ling

THE BIG WATER

The gorgeous Umiam Lake is locally called the Badapani Lake—meaning big water. It is a beautiful lake that is a part of a reservoir that was created when a dam was built on the Umiam river. There are lots of fun water sports organized here that visitors love.

Long, long ago

To know that, you'll have to understand Meghalaya's history. And it is an interesting history. So come along, let's peep into Meghalaya's past.

I wonder whether people lived here from the beginning of time or they came here from somewhere else.

THE STORY OF THREE TRIBES

Meghalaya's history is essentially the story of three tribes that have lived in this region for hundreds and hundreds of years. The Khasis, the Jaintias and the Garos are three tribes that happily lived together in these hills. They each had their own kingdom and were perfectly happy in their own worlds.

Khasi Warrior

JAINTIA KINGDOM

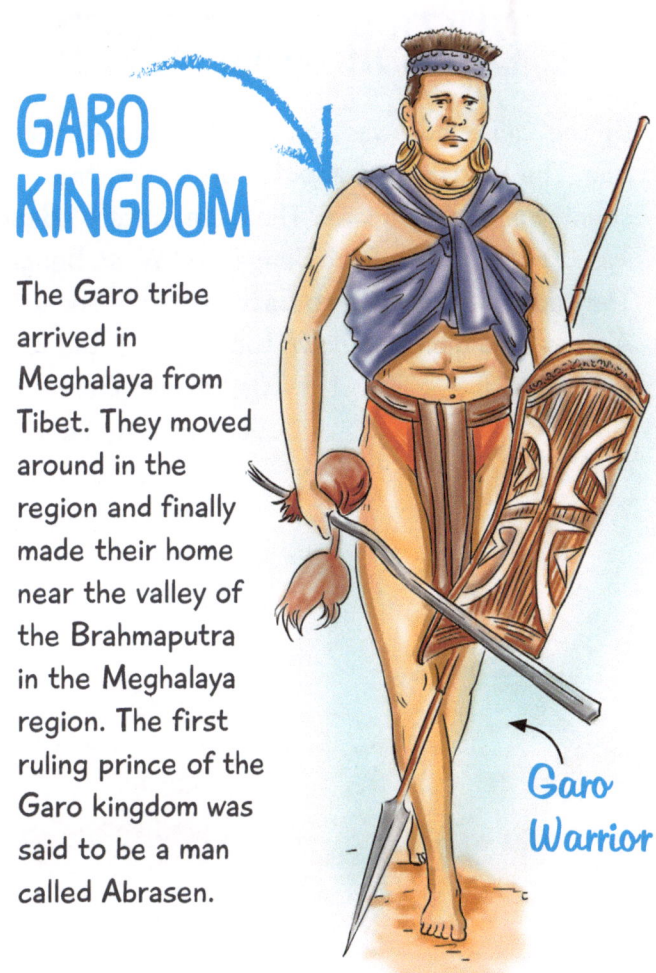

Silver coins of Jaintia kingdom

The Jaintia kingdom was established in the Jaintia Hills. Historians say that these tribes had a lot in common with Khasi tribes. Perhaps they had the same origins. The Jaintias were influenced by the Ahoms, a strong dynasty that ruled Assam.

GARO KINGDOM

The Garo tribe arrived in Meghalaya from Tibet. They moved around in the region and finally made their home near the valley of the Brahmaputra in the Meghalaya region. The first ruling prince of the Garo kingdom was said to be a man called Abrasen.

Garo Warrior

KHASI KINGDOMS

It is believed that the people of the Khasi tribe were the earliest inhabitants of Meghalaya. They wandered into this region from Burma (now Myanmar). Historians say there were more than twenty Khasi kingdoms—each tribe functioning on its own. They would war with each other and also attack settlers while trying to make a life for themselves.

A DEAL IS MADE

It so happened that the Burmese, who were looking to expand their kingdom, invaded the hills of Meghalaya. At the same time, the British, who had made India their colony, signed a treaty with the ruling Jaintia king, promising to protect the region. When the Burmese invaded, the British helped the Jaintia and Khasi kingdoms with their troops. In return, they wanted to build a route through Meghalaya so that they could carry on trading activities with Tibet and other countries.

THE BRITISH TAKE OVER

By this time, India was completely under British rule. The British went about reorganizing the country and making laws. The huge state of Bengal was broken up into East Bengal and West Bengal. They added Meghalaya to East Bengal, along with Assam. This didn't go down too well with the Khasi, Jaintia and Garo people. They began protesting—demanding that Meghalaya be a state in its own right.

U Khang Nongbeh was a Jaintia patriot who fought hard against the British rule.

Tirot Singh

TRIBAL REVOLT

The Jaintias decided to act. A freedom fighter called Tirot Singh started a full-fledged revolt. But the British were too strong for the simple tribals, who had no resources. They were soon overcome and had to step back.

STOPPING TRADE

All this while, people from the Khasi kingdom were conducting trade through a place called the Sylhet Market (now in Bangladesh). In order to control the region, the British took over the trade activities and stopped the Khasis from trading. They sent troops to guard the hills and make sure that the Khasis or Jaintias could not trade. This angered the tribal kingdoms even more.

WHAT'S ODD?

Mishki sees that there is one odd word in each row below. Can you find out which one that is?

| Revolt | Argue | Agree | Protest |

| Trade | Barter | Give | Exchange |

| Rules | Chaos | Laws | Regulations |

CALLING A TRUCE

The ill will between the British and the tribal kingdoms of the Meghalaya hills came to a brief stop. The British allowed a road to be built that allowed the people to move freely between different districts. The tribal kingdoms even signed a treaty with the British in which the British exempted them from paying taxes. This was a big relief to the people.

The British soldiers and traders from this region used this route.

TAKING THE GARO HILLS

The British had taken over the Khasi and Jaintia Hills, but they had still not managed to overcome the Garo Hills. The zamindars (landowners), in cahoots with the British, kept an eye on the Garo chiefs, making sure they didn't get out of hand. There were many fights between the zamindars and the tribal people. Finally, the British managed to take control of the Garo Hills as well.

The Garo natives fiercely defended their land.

INDIA BECOME INDEPENDENT

It wasn't only the tribals of Meghalaya who were unhappy with the way the British were ruling India, with unfair laws. People across the country were furious. They began to revolt. There were protests and riots, and after ruling India for more than 200 years, the British were finally forced to leave. In 1947, India became independent.

Indians protested for their freedom

A STATE IS BORN

Now the brand new Indian government had a new issue to tackle. They had to reorganize the country. They divided India into states, largely based on language. Assam became a state where Assamese was spoken. At this time, it included what is now Meghalaya. But the Khasi and Jaintia people wanted their own state and their own identity. They fought hard for it and finally, in 1972, Meghalaya was made a separate state.

HIDDEN WORDS

MEGHALAYA is such a big word. Can you make ten smaller English words from it?

M E G H A L A Y A

_____

_____ _____ _____

_____ _____

_____ _____

19

Talk time

What an interesting history! So, are there many languages spoken here?

Yes, the main tribes have their own languages, which are Khasi and Garo. Many people of the Jaintia tribe speak a language called Pnar.

OFFICIALLY ENGLISH

English is the official language in this state. Also, the English script used for both Khasi and Garo. There are many tribal dialects though that the various smaller tribes speak in. Tiwa and Biate are two such dialects. A lot of people also speak Nepali fluently.

PHRASES IN KHASI

English	Khasi
Hello	Kumno
How are you?	Phi long kumno?
I am fine	Nga biang
Thank you	Khublei
Yes	Hooid
No	Em
See you tomorrow	Sa lakynduh lashai
What is the time now?	Katno baje mynta?
Please	Sngewbha
Where?	Shano?
Where are you going?	Shano phin leit?
Sir/Mister	Bah
Miss/Madam	Kong
Bye	Khublei shibun

MATCH THE WORDS

Time to remember the new phrases. Can you match the Khasi words to their English meanings?

Please	Kumno
Where?	Nga biang
I am fine	Em
Hello	Khublei shibun
No	Sngewbha
Bye	Shano?

A peep into their life

Wow! I'd love to know more about all these colourful tribes and their lives.

Colourful is a good word to describe the culture of Meghalaya. You'll see lot of music, dance and, of course, colour.

TRIBAL TRENDS

Meghalaya, as we've seen, has many different tribes. The main three that have influenced the state's history are the Khasi, Jaintia and Garo tribes. But there are many smaller tribes too that are offshoots of these three main ones. Let's meet some.

KHASI

Khasi household

There are more than a million people of Khasi origin in Meghalaya. This is no longer a small tribe but a large community that has spread across Meghalaya and even Bangladesh. Many Khasi people were converted to Christianity by the missionaries who came to north-east India to spread the message of Christ. This is a clever tribe who built the famous root bridges of Cherrapunji that we'll see a little later.

GARO

This is the second largest tribe of Meghalaya. They call themselves the hill people and are very close to nature. While most of them are Christians, some of them have their own deities. They also pray to nature as well as animals. They believe that God created the Earth in eight days and he rested on the ninth day. The Garos used to live in deep forests and survived with their hunting skills.

JAINTIA

This tribe is also known as the Pnar or Synteng. The nobility of the Jaintias became Hindus or Christians, but many still follow their traditional religion called Niamtre. They have their own customs, festivals and dances that are all very colourful.

HAJONG

This is a smaller tribe, possibly the fourth largest in Meghalaya. People believe that they came into India from Tibet, which is why their customs, language and even features are similar to Tibetan people. Most Hajongs follow Hinduism and celebrate many Hindu festivals like Durga Puja.

TIWA PEOPLE

Also called Lalung, this tribe lives in the hills as well as the plains. The hill Tiwas speak a version of the Garo language, while those on the plains speak Assamese.

ROCK ON!

Because there are so many tribes, Meghalaya has many types of lovely dances and music too! The folk songs are mostly about love, birth, marriage, nature and, of course, God. The people play traditional musical instruments like the *duitara*, and others that are similar to drums, flutes and cymbals.

Did you know?
Meghalaya has a very strong culture of rock music. There are some famous rock concerts, both Indian and international, that are held here.

A SPRING DANCE

The *ka shad suk mynsiem* is a dance that tribal people perform to celebrate harvest and the sowing season. The boys and girls (usually only unmarried ones participate) wear the most colourful outfits when they do this dance.

SPIN AWAY!

Chambil mesara or the pomelo dance needs amazing skill. A single performer dangles a pomelo (or any other fruit) from a rope he ties around his waist. Then he begins to spin the pomelo, faster and faster—without seeming to move his hips or his body! Some dancers can spin many fruits at the same time.

TURBAN KNOCK

The *doregata* is a really fun dance during which the female dancers have to knock off the turbans of their partners while dancing. As you can imagine, there is much cheering, clapping and laughter as the audience eggs on the dancers and thoroughly enjoys this dance.

LOVELY LAHOO

Lahoo is a dance that both men and women perform. It's done mainly for entertainment. There's always a lead performer who recites a couplet, and the followers who dance to it.

FESTIVALS FUN

The people from Meghalaya simply love to celebrate. Right from births, to marriages, to changing seasons . . . everything is celebrated with festive music, dance and food.

THE DANCE OF THE JOYFUL HEART

Shad suk mynsiem is an important ten-day-long Khasi festival also called the 'dance of the joyful heart'. It's basically a festival during which people give thanks for all that they have. People wear bright, traditional clothes and dance, sing and enjoy yummy food.

A HOUSE-WARMING CELEBRATION

Ka-shad-kynjoh khaskain is a house-warming celebration. There are special rituals and prayers held, after which a dance is performed that starts in the evening and goes on till dawn.

People make huge towers of paper and cardboard that symbolize trees.

SOW SOW SOW THE SEEDS

Behdienkhlam is a Jaintia festival that is celebrated after the sowing period is over. Young men beat the roof of every house with bamboo poles to drive away evil spirits. Then the pole is placed across a stream, and two groups compete to grab it, dancing in muddy pools of water. Sounds like fun!

WORD JUMBLE

Pushka needs to unjumble the words in order to remember what he's learned about Meghalaya's culture and people. Help him out, please.

1. This dancer is skilful at spinning a _____ (OMPEOL) tied at his waist.

2. In the doregata dance, the women try and knock off the partners' _____ (UTRANBS)

3. The _____ (ARGO) is the second largest tribe in Meghalaya.

4. Ka-shad-kynjoh khaskain is a _____ (USHEO)-warming celebration.

HONOURING THE DEAD

Mangona or *Chugana* is a ceremony held after the funeral of a person. As a part of the ritual, performers (usually family members) sing and dance all through the night. A special kinds of meal is cooked for everyone. It's a sombre occasion, but one that helps bring peace to the family.

DANCE OF HUNDRED DRUMS

The *Wangala* is an important Garo festival. Every November, for an entire week, tribal farmers celebrate the end of their sowing season. They pray for a good harvest. They pray to a god called Satyong. Dressed in traditional costumes and feathered head-dresses, young and old dancers get together and stomp to the beat of a hundred drums.

Nongkrem Dance Festival

THANKING GOD WITH A DANCE

Khasi tribes celebrate the Nongkrem Dance Festival for five whole days—mainly to thank the gods for a good harvest. All through the five days, music is played and the younger people dance together. Men hold a sword in their hands as they dance. This symbolizes that they are keeping their families safe from evil.

THE DOVE DANCE

O'Kru sua is a dance in which people celebrate nature and birds. The dance is performed by two dancers who mimic the way doves peck at each other. Of course, the audience finds this funny and thoroughly enjoys the performance. This dance reflects how close the tribal people are to nature.

TWIN DOVES

Mishki loves the dove dance. Can you help her find the twin of the dove shown here?

A   B   C

D   E   F

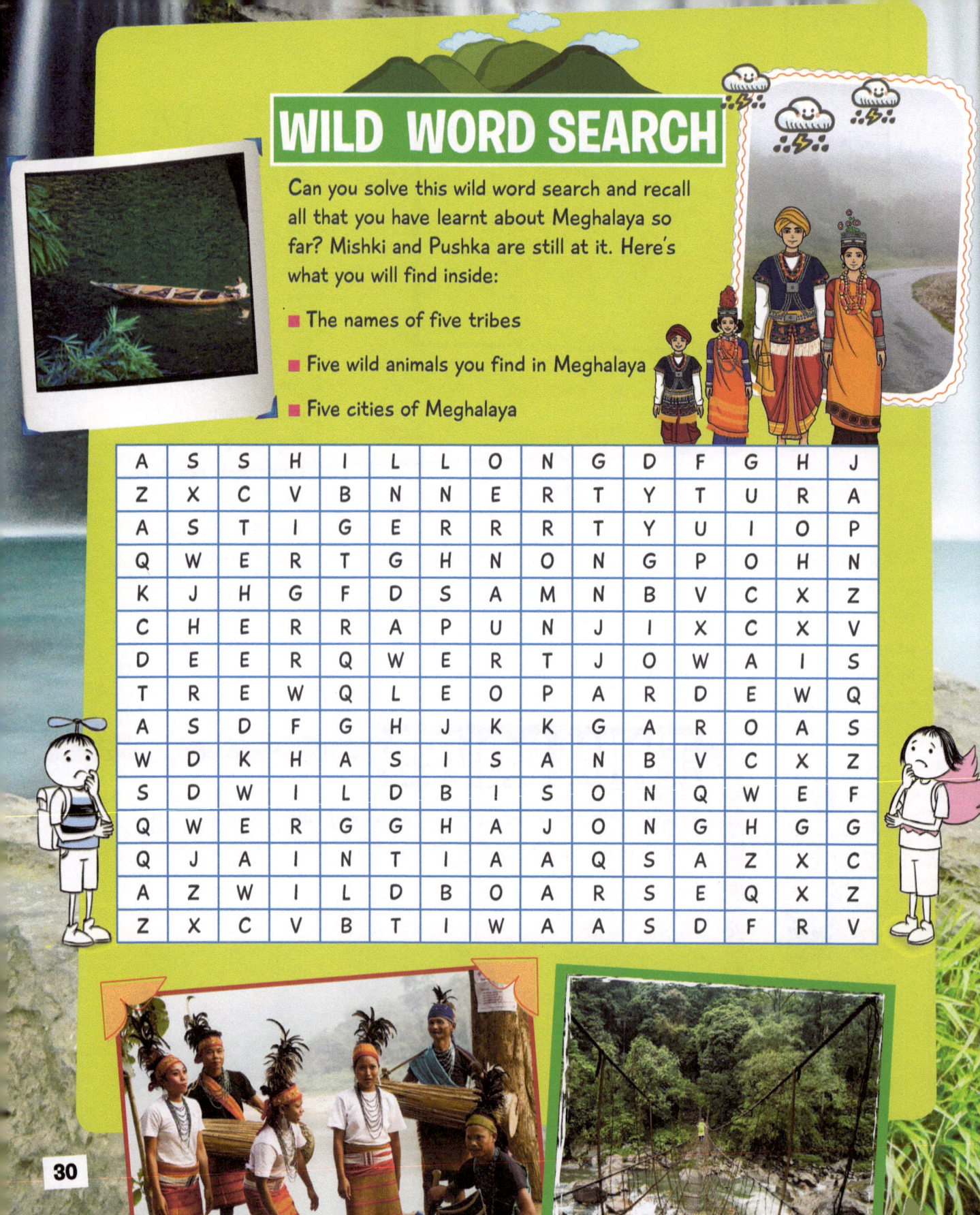

WILD WORD SEARCH

Can you solve this wild word search and recall all that you have learnt about Meghalaya so far? Mishki and Pushka are still at it. Here's what you will find inside:

- The names of five tribes
- Five wild animals you find in Meghalaya
- Five cities of Meghalaya

A	S	S	H	I	L	L	O	N	G	D	F	G	H	J
Z	X	C	V	B	N	N	E	R	T	Y	T	U	R	A
A	S	T	I	G	E	R	R	R	T	Y	U	I	O	P
Q	W	E	R	T	G	H	N	O	N	G	P	O	H	N
K	J	H	G	F	D	S	A	M	N	B	V	C	X	Z
C	H	E	R	R	A	P	U	N	J	I	X	C	X	V
D	E	E	R	Q	W	E	R	T	J	O	W	A	I	S
T	R	E	W	Q	L	E	O	P	A	R	D	E	W	Q
A	S	D	F	G	H	J	K	K	G	A	R	O	A	S
W	D	K	H	A	S	I	S	A	N	B	V	C	X	Z
S	D	W	I	L	D	B	I	S	O	N	Q	W	E	F
Q	W	E	R	G	G	H	A	J	O	N	G	H	G	G
Q	J	A	I	N	T	I	A	A	Q	S	A	Z	X	C
A	Z	W	I	L	D	B	O	A	R	S	E	Q	X	Z
Z	X	C	V	B	T	I	W	A	A	S	D	F	R	V

CRAZY CROSSWORD

Mishki and Pushka have learnt so much. They want to see how much they remember. Can you help them solve this giant crossword?

ACROSS

1. Something soft and fluffy after which Meghalaya has been named.
3. They ruled India with an iron hand for the longest time.
5. This bird is known to be very proud. Oh yes, you find it in Meghalaya.
7. Meghalaya was once a part of this state.
8. Something hard, something musical. Shillong is famous for this type of concerts.
9. Deep, dark cavities in mountainsides. Meghalaya has plenty of them.
10. They gush and rush and leap into rivers.
13. This fruit is hung at the waist of a Meghalayan dancer.
16. A famous tribe from Meghalaya.
17. A bird whose name sounds like a device used to honk.
18. A pretty bird that pecks its beak with other birds like itself. It has inspired a dance too.

DOWN

2. Spot its spots and you'll have seen an amazing animal.
4. Meghalaya has six of these siblings.
6. It rains and pours and never seems to stop here.
11. A tiny tribe from Meghalaya that rhymes with Java.
12. It's green, it squawks and it flies around Meghalaya's forests.
14. A name for a fruit farm.
15. They attacked Meghalaya and tried to build a kingdom there.

Bricks and stones

I wonder what kind of houses the tribal people built. It must have been hard—living in forests, moving around from place to place.

Tribal people, you will see, are very creative and resourceful. They are used to making the most of what they have. The houses you see in Meghalaya are just that— simple, but very creative.

Traditional Garo home

GARO HOUSES

The Garo tribes built their homes using what was available to them—timber, cane, bamboo and wood from rubber trees and dried palm leaves. The tradition was that each man built a home for his family, using the tribe's help. The younger people, even children, helped out so that they too learnt how to build their own house for when the time came. The spaces are nicely allocated in a Garo home. The living room, called a *dongrama*, has a fireplace. The rooms are usually in a long line, with a porch and a cowshed for the family cow.

HOMES WITH A PURPOSE

There are many kinds of houses in Meghalaya—each with a different purpose.

Nokpante is a dormitory-style house in which bachelors and young men live.

Jamsreng is a house where grains and fruits are stored.

Borang are smaller houses, often built on treetops, to keep families safe from wild animals.

Jamatal are houses built in the middle of fields.

KHASI CREATIVITY

The Khasi tribes live in areas that are highly earthquake-prone. They need to make sure their houses are light and easy to build, so that when there is an earthquake, no one gets hurt if a house collapses, and rebuilding the house takes no time at all. The houses are built on raised platforms so that even if the earth shakes, the stilts absorb the shock.

RHYME TIME

Can you think of three words to rhyme with the ones Mishki has given here?

EARTHQUAKE _____ _____ _____

PLATFORM _____ _____ _____

TREETOP _____ _____ _____

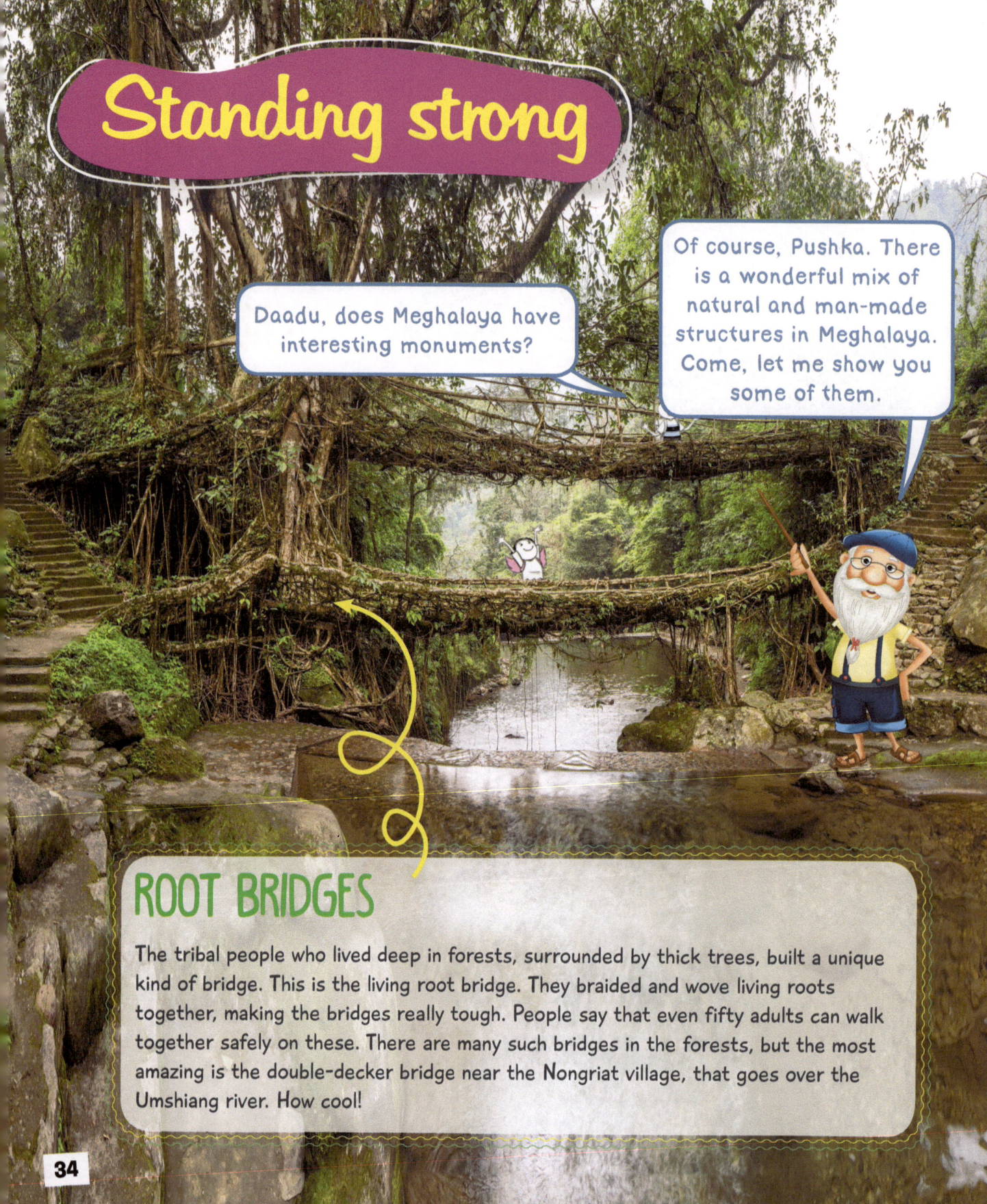

Standing strong

Daadu, does Meghalaya have interesting monuments?

Of course, Pushka. There is a wonderful mix of natural and man-made structures in Meghalaya. Come, let me show you some of them.

ROOT BRIDGES

The tribal people who lived deep in forests, surrounded by thick trees, built a unique kind of bridge. This is the living root bridge. They braided and wove living roots together, making the bridges really tough. People say that even fifty adults can walk together safely on these. There are many such bridges in the forests, but the most amazing is the double-decker bridge near the Nongriat village, that goes over the Umshiang river. How cool!

BRIDGING THE GAP

The tribes built stone bridges too to help them cross rivers. There are many megalithic bridges scattered across the state. The bridge across the Um Kumbeh river is one such. Can you imagine the people building this bridge themselves, lifting heavy stones?

MEMORIALS MADE OF STONE

These megalithic stone memorials were made hundreds of years ago in memory of people who had died fighting, especially tribal heroes. Some of these are menhirs, some are dolmens and some are cairns. Many of them are gigantic. The U Maw Thodur-Briew and U-Mawthoh-Dur are some of the famous ones that people interested in history come to gaze at.

Wow! I want to build a megalithic structure.

A megalith is an enormous single piece of stone. Menhirs, dolmens and cairns are stones which are of specific shapes. A menhir is oval and pointed towards the top, a dolmen is a flattish stone and cairns are a pile of smaller stones.

A TANK WITH A DIFFERENCE

This is a simple tank, made special by how old it is. The Jaintia kings are said to have ordered this to be carved out of granite rock thousands of years ago. A beautifully carved stone elephant head sits at one edge. It seems as if the elephant is drinking water from the tank. People must have used this tank for bathing all those years ago.

DAVID SCOTT'S MONUMENT

David Scott was an officer of the British government. He must have been popular because there is a monument in his honour that people visit even today. It's a simple monument shaped like an obelisk. When you visit it and read the inscription, you are transported right back into time.

DON BOSCO SQUARE

This square in Shillong has an unusual story. At the heart of the square stands the statue of Don Bosco, a missionary. He was known to be an educator and friend of the young people. Now this has become a hangout spot for young students.

THE MONUMENT OF FRANCE

This monument in Shillong is dedicated to Khasi soldiers who died during World War I. They fought as a part of the British army in France. Imagine the journey! Simple tribal people, from a corner of India, fighting for the British! Known locally as Motphran, the monument is now in a bustling part of town.

THE CATHEDRAL OF MARY HELP OF CHRISTIANS

There were many Catholic missionaries who came to the north-east of India to spread the message of Jesus Christ. They built many churches. One of the most famous is the Cathedral of Mary Help of Christians in Shillong. The unique thing about this church is that it has been built on sand. The architects cut deep holes in rock, filled it with sand and then built the church on it. This way, during earthquakes, the sand absorbs the shock and protects the building.

MONUMENT MATCH

Mishki and Pushka are monument-spotting. Can you find the picture and name of each monument and where it is? Remember, there are monuments from Meghalaya as well as from other parts of India and the world.

Statue of Liberty

1

 **Egypt**

Eiffel Tower

4

2

 **China**

Taj Mahal

5

 **Greece**

Monument of France

Big Ben

 **USA**

 **Brazil**

Pyramids

 **Meghalaya**

3

6

France

Great Wall of China

Egypt

10

London

Christ the Redeemer

7

Meghalaya

8

11

Sphinx

Little Mermaid

Cathedral of Mary Help of Christians

India

12

England

Stonehenge

Acropolis

9

Denmark

13

Working hard

I wish I was a tribal who lived in Meghalaya. I rather like their life.

Well, if you were a tribal person, you would have to work hard, as they all do even now. Would you like to know what kind of work people do in Meghalaya today?

Yes, please!

TOURIST TREND

Tourism is a big industry in Meghalaya because of its natural beauty.

The water is so clear in the Umngot river that you can see the bottom.

Workers inside coal mine

MINERAL MIGHT

Meghalaya has a lot of minerals, like limestone, coal and granite, in its soil. There are many quarries where people work to get these minerals out of the ground.

FARMER, FARMER, WHAT DO YOU GROW?

Agriculture is the most important occupation in Meghalaya. Most people work either as farmers, or in businesses to do with making things from farm produce. Rice is one of the most important crops. There are many fruit orchards too, because the weather is perfect for oranges, guava, jackfruit and bananas. The farmers have to cope with sloping land and need to cut into the slopes and make terrace farms. Or they burn forests to clear land.

FLOWERS, FLOWERS EVERYWHERE

The climate of Meghalaya is perfect for flowers. Apart from wild flowers, there are people who cultivate flowers to sell them. This is called floriculture. People grow orchids, dahlias, asters, begonias and many other lovely flowers that are sold across the country.

Floriculturist in Khasi Hills

WEAVING MAGIC

The weavers of Meghalaya weave magic with the silk that is made here. *Eri* silk is unique to this place. Mixed with wool, the shawls that the weavers create are warm and wonderful. Usually women take this on and add to the family income.

Worker at a silk farm

BREEDING SILKWORMS

The silk of Meghalaya is famous. There are many silk farms where people breed silkworms. This is a tough job because the entire process is very delicate and complicated. But it does give rise to wonderful, soft-as-cloud silk.

EXOTIC EMBROIDERY

Some regions of Meghalaya are famous for their wonderful embroidery. Called *khneng* embroidery, this intricate style actually depicts the trading routes of Meghalaya. Isn't that amazing? This is a famous style that people from across the world love.

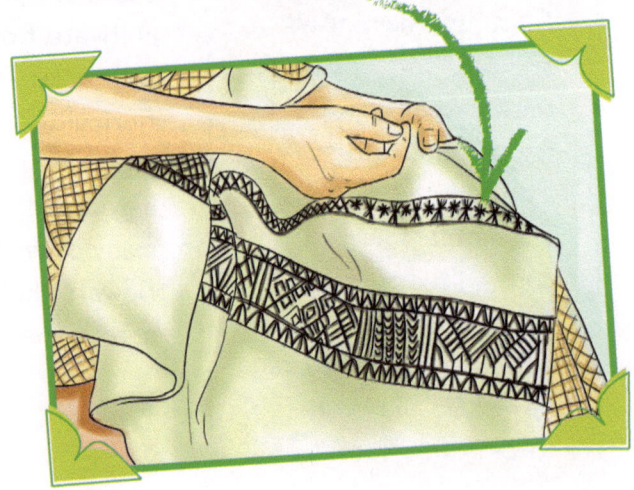

HANDY HANDICRAFTS

The craftsmen of Meghalaya are especially skilful at weaving amazing objects of cane and bamboo. They make baskets, mats, trays, bowls and many other things that tourists buy.

Bamboo craftswomen

Time to DRAW

Mishki has drawn a lovely cane basket. Can you copy it?

Draw here

Yum yum yum

You have been ready for a while now, Pushka. So I won't make you wait any more. Come on and let's taste some of Meghalaya's amazing food.

My favourite part, Daadu. I have my fork and knife all ready. Are we going to taste the food now?

ALL SORTS OF FOOD

The cuisine of Meghalaya is a tasty mix of different styles of cooking. The various tribes have their own specialties. There is a lot of meat in this cuisine because these people lived as hunter-gatherers.

JADOH JOY

This is a very popular dish made of red rice cooked along with different meats. It's a spicy dish with plenty of chillies. It has a lovely yellow colour and amazing fragrance, and you can't stop until you've eaten it all.

YES TO NAKHMAM BITCHI

This is a soup that people have before their meals. Nakhmam is a river fish, which is dried in the sun (or over a fire. It is then boiled to make a thick soup. The soup is very spicy, so be careful lest you gulp it down.

DIVINE DOH-NEIIONG

This is a hot favourite with the locals. It's a super-rich, super-tasty meat curry full of all kinds of spices and flavours. Sesame seeds are the hero of this dish and add a crunch to the heavenly taste.

PUMALOI PERFECTION

Pumaloi means powdered rice. This popular dish is made by steaming the rice powder in a special pot. It's a tricky dish to make because the cook has to use an exact amount of water and an exact amount of heat. But once it's ready, it's delicious. It's like a pancake that people thoroughly enjoy.

PUDOH PARTY

Here's another dish made of powdered rice. But this time, lots of meat and spices are added to this, and the final outcome is a very tasty dish. It's one of the staples of wedding menus and a much-loved dish.

SAVOURY SAKIN GATA

This is a rice cake that's mixed with sugar and made in layers, served on banana leaves. It's served piping hot, so mind that you don't burn your tongue.

Jaggery

YUMMY PUKHLEIN

Powdered rice seems to be something that people here love. This is made nice and sweet with lots of jaggery. Some people like to eat it by itself, but it's also eaten along with other meat dishes.

TASTY TUNGRYMBAI

This is a popular tribal dish eaten now by the rural folk. It is very nutritious and made of beans, meat and sesame, and people have it almost every day.

DISHY DOHKHLIEH

Salad time! This delicious salad is made of meat, onion and chillies. Chefs also get creative sometimes by adding beans, tomatoes and carrots. Hmmm! Sounds healthy! People say this dish is good for the skin.

MMMMMM... MINIL SONGA

Here's a dish that is as tasty as it is healthy. It's made of a sticky rice with a yummy nutty flavour which is then mixed with bamboo. What you get is a meal that helps keep your tummy clean and your digestive system in good condition.

CRACK THE **FOOD** CODE

Can you help Pushka crack the food code so that he can fill his tummy with the yummy food he's read about?

I = 2	L = 3	C = 7	E = 10
T = 1	U = 4	H = 9	Y = 11
S = 5	N = 6	M = 8	

2 5   2 1   3 4 6 7 9 1 2 8 10   11 10 1

What to wear?

The tribal clothes I have been seeing are unusual, Daadu. Does everyone wear them?

Well, there are the traditional tribal clothes people wear during special occasions like festivals and weddings. You'll see that the various tribes usually wear a long piece of colourful cloth draped in different styles.

KHASI SPLENDOUR

The men of the Khasi tribes wear a simple long cloth around their waist, much like a dhoti. They team this with a jacket and a turban, or some other headgear.

The women wear a long cloth like a sarong, called a *jainsen*. On top of their blouses, they wear a cotton shawl—like an apron—called a *tap-moh khlieh*. During festivals, they dress up beautifully with elaborate jewellery.

GARO STYLES

Depending on where they live, Garo women dress differently. The hills see women wearing a cloth called *eking* around their waist. In the more crowded areas, they wear a long cloth like a lungi, called a *dakmanda*, with a blouse.

Men wear a simple cloth wrapped around their waist and chest as their traditional dress. During festivals, they add on interesting headgear and jewellery too!

Jaintia couple

JAINTIA JOY

The Jaintia women wear a sarong similar to the Khasi sarong, called a *thohk khyrwang*. They sometimes cover their heads with a small checked cloth called a *kyrshah*. The men's clothes are similar to what Khasi men wear.

MARRIAGE MAGNIFICENCE

Look at this bride and groom all dressed up for their wedding. Can you spot ten differences in the two pictures?

49

Autograph, please?

> The people of Meghalaya must have had to struggle hard to achieve things. Is that true?

> Well, yes, in a way that is true. Especially the tribal people. But you will be amazed at how much they have done. There are some amazing achievers who hail from Meghalaya. Let's meet some of them.

BERTHA GYNDYKES DKHAR

She is an educationist who is blind. She lost her eyesight when she was in college. But not only did she complete her education, she even created Braille in Khasi. Isn't that amazing? She's won the Padma Shri—one of India's highest awards.

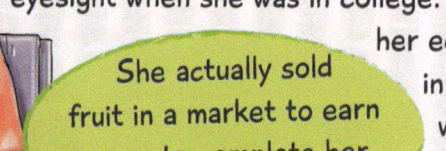

She actually sold fruit in a market to earn money to complete her studies.

HAMLET BAREH NGAPKYNTA

He was a writer, film director and historian who was the first person from a Khasi tribe to get a PhD. He also made the first-ever feature film in Khasi. He won many awards for his amazing work.

HELEN GIRI SYIEM

This interesting woman helped bring Khasi music to the world. Because of her efforts, the tradition of Khasi music was kept alive. She is known to be a descendant of a Meghalaya royal family.

LOU MAJAW

Here's a true rock star. Lou Majaw is a guitarist and rock musician who rose from a very humble background. He taught himself the guitar and now performs in rock concerts all over India, where thousands of young people come to hear him.

VERNA ELIZABETH WATRE INGTY

She was a social worker from the Garo tribe who worked hard for the betterment of the tribal people, and for society at large. She won the Padma Shri award for her lifelong efforts.

Once upon a time . . .

Imagine sitting and watching these beautiful hills and listening to a story about this lovely state.

If you are dropping a hint that I should tell you a story... then the hint has worked. Settle down and I'll tell you a folk tale about the god of Shillong.

THE LEGEND OF THE SHILLONG PEAK

The ancient Khasis were fascinated with the Shillong peak. It was the highest peak in the land and no one had ever been there. The simple tribal people believed that God lived in the mountains. But they didn't know how to worship Him, for no one had ever seen Him or even knew how to get there.

One day, a man called U Shillong, who was wiser than the others, told them, 'Come, I will tell you how to pray to the god on the peak,' he said. He showed them how to make garlands. He taught them prayers.

But he didn't tell them the name of the god. So they began to call the god U Lei Shillong (which meant the god of U Shillong). And that is how Shillong got its name.

But the story does not end here.

The god on the mountain had three beautiful daughters. Two of the daughters transformed themselves into rivers and came to Earth to look after the Khasi people. But one daughter decided to turn herself into a little girl. She came to earth and sat quietly on a tall rock.

A group of young shepherd boys, who were minding their sheep, suddenly saw the beautiful child sitting on the rock. They were astounded. They had been trying to climb that rock for years but no one had succeeded. How had this delicate little girl done it?

'Did you see that girl sitting up on the rock?' one boy called.

'Impossible! No one can climb that rock,' exclaimed another. 'It must be a spirit.' Scared, all the boys ran home to tell the village elders about the strange sight.

At first the elders didn't believe them.

'Don't make up stories,' they scolded the boys. 'No one can climb that rock.'

But they agreed to go and see for themselves. When they got there, they couldn't believe their eyes. A little girl, with such beauty as they had never seen before, sat on the rock.

'We must get her down,' one villager said.

'Yes, she must be scared all by herself,' added another. They saw that the girl was dressed differently from all of them. Her clothes were richer and her jewellery finer.

Finally, one man called U Mylliem Ngap, who was as strong as he was wise, thought of a way. He made a tall, tall ladder with a whole lot of bamboo trees. Then he climbed up all the way to the top. The child refused to move.

U Mylliem Ngap thought of another idea. He collected a bunch of beautiful wild flowers and climbed up again. He held the flowers out to the girl.

When the girl saw the flowers, she smiled. She reached out for them. U Mylliem Ngap stepped down, one rung at a time. The girl followed him and soon she was safely on the ground.

It was decided that since he had rescued her, U Mylliem Ngap would become her father. He named her Pah Syntiew—which means 'the one who was lured by flowers'.

Pah Syntiew grew up to be a beautiful maiden. She too was wise like her father. She was also very talented. She taught the other maidens of the tribe lovely songs and dances. She began to solve people's problems, and people from other villages began to come to consult her.

Soon it was time for her marriage. She was married to a man called U Kongor Nongjri. The couple was happy. They had many lovely children.

Finally one day, Pah Syntiew told her children the secret of her birth. She told them that her real father was U Lei Shillong, the mountain god, and that he had sent her to earth to bring joy to people and teach them a new way of life.

'But now, it is time for me to go back,' she said.

Hearing this, the villagers all fell at her feet. They begged her not to go, but her time had come. She walked away into a cave and was never seen again. But the songs and dances she taught the people are still danced and sung. And they say that her ancestors became the two leading families of the Khasis—the Khairim and Mylliem.

The story of Pah Syntiew is still told to children by their mothers and grandmothers.

TRAVEL DIARY

Have you enjoyed this trip to Meghalaya with your friends Mishki and Pushka—and, of course, with Daadu Dolma?

Now you can make your own Meghalaya diary. And if you ever visit Meghalaya, make sure you take pictures and put them in the photo box.

The first place I would visit in Meghalaya:

_____

If I were a farmer, I would grow:

_____

The one dish I am definitely going to eat:

_____

The monument I think is the most interesting:

_____

The one famous person from Meghalaya I would love to meet:

_____

I think the most interesting historical figure from Meghalaya is:

_____

The festival from Meghalaya that I think is the most fun:

_____

The five words that I think describe Meghalaya the best are:

_____

_____

_____

_____

_____

My Meghalaya memories:

ANSWERS

Page 7 RHYME TIME

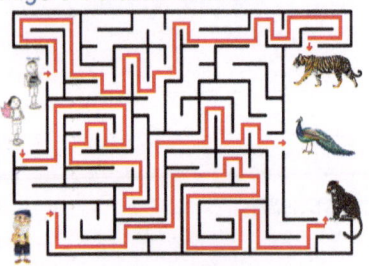

G	P	R	O	U	D	F	D	S	A
V	O	W	E	D	C	X	C	V	B
C	C	O	W	E	D	W	X	F	Q
V	V	C	R	O	W	D	D	E	S
Z	X	V	B	A	L	O	U	D	A
L	O	U	D	N	M	Z	A	S	D
A	C	B	O	W	E	D	Z	X	C
P	L	O	U	G	H	E	D	Q	S

Page 9 FOREST SAFARI

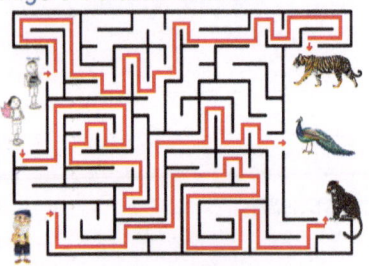

Page 17 WHAT'S ODD?

AGREE, GIVE, CHAOS

Page 19 HIDDEN WORDS

Here are some of the words you can form:
age, ale, elm, gel, gym, ham, hay, lag, lay,
leg, may, yam, gala, gale, game, glam, hale,
heal, lame, meal

Page 21 MATCH THE WORDS

Please—Sngewbha; Where?—Shano; I am
fine—Nga biang; Hello—Kumno; No—Em;
Bye—Khublei shibun

Page 27 WORD JUMBLE

1. Pomelo 2. Turbans 3. Garo 4. House

Page 29 TWIN DOVES

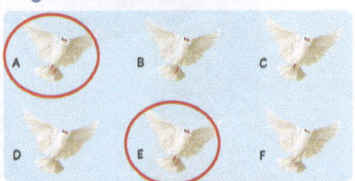

Page 30 WILD WORD SEARCH

A	S	S	H	I	L	L	O	N	G	D	F	G	H	J
Z	X	C	V	B	N	N	E	R	T	Y	T	U	R	A
A	S	T	T	I	G	E	R	R	R	T	Y	U	I	O
Q	W	E	R	T	G	H	N	O	N	G	P	O	H	N
K	J	H	G	F	D	S	A	M	N	B	V	C	X	Z
C	H	E	R	R	A	P	U	N	J	I	X	C	X	V
U	E	R	Q	W	E	R	T	J	O	W	A	I	S	G
T	R	E	W	Q	L	E	O	P	A	R	D	E	W	Q
A	S	D	F	G	H	J	K	K	G	A	R	O	S	D
W	D	K	H	A	S	I	S	A	N	B	V	C	X	Z
S	D	W	I	L	D	B	I	S	O	N	Q	W	E	F
Q	W	E	R	G	G	H	A	J	O	N	G	H	G	G
Q	J	A	I	N	T	I	A	A	Q	S	A	Z	X	C
A	Z	W	I	L	D	B	O	A	R	S	E	Q	X	Z
Z	X	C	V	B	T	I	W	A	A	S	D	F	R	V

Page 31 CRAZY CROSSWORD

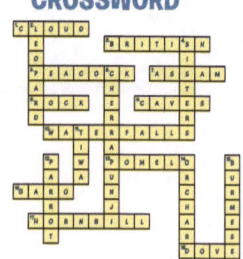

Page 33 RHYME TIME

backache, handshake, mistake; brainstorm,
hailstorm, inform; chop, crop, hop

Page 38–39 MONUMENT MATCH

1. The Big Ben, England
2. Acropolis, Greece
3. Christ the Redeemer, Brazil
4. The Great Wall of China, China
5. The Stonehenge, England
6. The Sphinx, Egypt
7. The Taj Mahal, Agra
8. The Statue of Liberty, USA
9. The Eiffel Tower, France
10. Monument of France, Meghalaya
11. Little Mermaid, Denmark
12. The Great Pyramids, Egypt
13. Cathedral of Mary Help of Christians, Meghalaya

Page 47 CRACK THE FOOD CODE

IS IT LUNCHTIME YET?

Page 49 MARRIAGE MAGNIFICENCE